IMAGES
of America

THE HYDE-MURPHY COMPANY

The Hyde-Murphy Company was an architectural business that erected and decorated buildings all over the country, including many prominent public buildings in Washington, DC. It started as a lumber sawmill, then added specialty woodwork, glass, and materials. It is responsible for many beautiful mansions, known as the "lilies of the valley" in Elk County. This beautiful train station example carries the name of the firm's hometown, Ridgway, Pennsylvania. (Dennis McGeehan.)

On the Cover: This hub of activity is the Hyde-Murphy Company in Ridgway. From this site, world-famous architectural products flowed to the local area and the nation. The company's interior woodwork decorated the Library of Congress, the Supreme Court, the Pentagon, and the Smithsonian Institution in Washington, DC. These workers are busy inhaling the intoxication of American ingenuity and artistry, as well as sawdust and real old-fashioned horsepower. (Courtesy of Elk County Historical Society.)

IMAGES
of America

THE HYDE-MURPHY COMPANY

Dennis McGeehan

ARCADIA
PUBLISHING

ISBN 978-1-4671-0681-8

Published by Arcadia Publishing
Charleston, South Carolina

Printed in the United States of America

Library of Congress Control Number: 2020952423

For all general information, please contact Arcadia Publishing:
Telephone 843-853-2070
Fax 843-853-0044
E-mail sales@arcadiapublishing.com
For customer service and orders:
Toll-Free 1-888-313-2665

Visit us on the Internet at www.arcadiapublishing.com

This book is dedicated to Deb, wife and life.

Contents

ACKNOWLEDGMENTS

I would like to thank the following for their help in the production of this book. Debra Shaw McGeehan for her tireless work in retyping, spellchecking, image preparation, and overall oversight; Caitrin Cunningham for her patience and encouragement; Bob Imhof and Dale Fox and members of the Ridgway Heritage Council for their support; the Elk County Historical Society for their image collection and archives; the St. Marys & Benzinger Township Historical Society; Mike Heiberger; Pete Winklbauer; Bill Bauer for his knowledge of railroads; and Mark Wendel for the use of his extensive collection of historical postcard images. Photographs of modern buildings for comparison were taken by the author, Dennis McGeehan.

Images in this volume appear courtesy of the Elk County Historical Society (EC), St. Marys & Benzinger Township Historical Society (SM), Mark Wendel (MW), and Dennis McGeehan.

INTRODUCTION

The first pioneers reaching Ridgway found woods, which were an obstacle. They had no idea that wood would eventually become Ridgway's salvation and signature product. Turning wood into architecture and art made Ridgway famous.

Ridgway is the county seat of Elk County, located on Elk Creek, flowing into the Clarion River at Ridgway. The name *Clarion* means loud, clear, ringing, and inspiring. Elk County is named after the majestic elk. The last native elk was killed along the Clarion River in 1867; elk have since been reintroduced, becoming a major tourist industry in the county.

Air currents in the northern hemisphere mostly move from west to east. Air masses flow up the Mississippi and Ohio River Valleys, increasing in height and moisture with every mile. As they rise, they drop moisture as rain. That is why we have the Allegheny National Forest. The moist air propagates evergreen and deciduous forests in the Allegheny Mountains, finally arriving in Ridgway, which is redolent of trees and wood. Moisture creates creeks, branches, rivers, and sometimes floods. At times, the air has even smelled of fire. (Bear Creek, just west of Ridgway, was the scene of a huge forest fire in 1926.) The earth, air, and water gave Ridgway resources and a delivery system. Ridgway sent its stylish product to the world. Today, artists flow into Ridgway to complete a grand cycle. Tourism, recreation, and history are today's artifice.

Around 450 BC, the ancient Greek Empedocles posited four elements in the universe: earth, wind, fire, and water. The Elk County pioneers found these elements. They found earth, covered with wood. Wood moved down the hillsides into Ridgway. The agent of this delivery was the lumberjack. The tools were the double-bitted ax and crosscut saw. Another element was water. Elk County is atop the mid-continental divide, where streams flow toward the Atlantic Ocean via the Susquehanna River, or toward the Gulf of Mexico via the Allegheny, Ohio, and Mississippi Rivers. Water moved wood downstream to sawmills. Ridgway lumber baron Joseph Smith Hyde floated his timber to a sawmill in Freeport owned by Walter P. Murphy. This partnership proved so fruitful that Murphy moved to Ridgway to incorporate a woodworking business with Hyde.

Wood flowed into Ridgway to the Hyde-Murphy Company. It was met with band saws, jigsaws, scroll saws, veneer saws, lathes, milling machines, miters, and routers. Construction and craft flowed out of this factory. As Bob Dylan sang, "As I went out one morning to breathe the air around Tom Paine," this was a brand-new air, vinted in 1776 and known as American air. This air held liberty and the freedom to create. American freedom bred invention and art. Americans sought new directions, not afraid of the past or the future. They tasted the air of freedom and created communities. That air engaged all five senses. It was the smell of sawdust, the sight of wilderness, the feel of tools, the sound of axes, and the taste of freedom. American air tasted of liberty, hard work, invention, and design. Style flowed out of the Hyde-Murphy Company. It flowed far and wide. The company built structures and decorated buildings with high-quality woodwork. Henry C. Park breathed liberally of the American air. Park was Hyde-Murphy's resident architect. He rejected the conservative norms of the past and designed new and unique homes with distinctive, unique millwork. His beautiful work can still be seen in many of the mansions of Ridgway.

Hyde-Murphy built in Ridgway and around the country and was especially active in Washington, DC. The company's signature beautiful woodwork can be found in the Library of Congress, the Pentagon, the Supreme Court, the Smithsonian Institution, and several foreign embassies.

In 1910, the final Greek element, fire, created a Greek tragedy. A huge blaze destroyed most of the factory and its many buildings, all made of wood. The fire consumed the physical plant and burned through the block to Ridgway's Main Street and destroyed a large section of the business district. The company immediately decided to rebuild, and within two years was up and running again in new buildings made of brick. The firm continued to serve its customers until closing in 1961.

Today, Ridgway has reinvented itself as a tourism mecca. Ridgway is located in two separate tourism regions: the Lumber Heritage Region and the Pennsylvania Wilds. It is in the Allegheny National Forest and along the Clarion River National Wild & Scenic River. Modern air is about enjoying outdoor bounty and conservation. Canoeing, wildlife, history, and wilderness all come together in Ridgway. The Hyde-Murphy Company built many mansions for lumber barons and wealthy citizens throughout Ridgway. These mansions gave rise to a nickname: "Lily of the Valley." These "lilies" are outstanding examples of period construction, making Ridgway a destination for lovers of materials, design, and planning.

The history of Ridgway flows seamlessly from then to now. The Hyde-Murphy Company is gone, but its influence is stamped on the town. Walk down its streets and admire the elegant structures. Linger on Main Street and admire the grand facades of the historic district. Be impressed by the stately courthouse. Elk Creek and the Clarion River flow through the regenerated forest. Canoe, bicycle, or hike around the county to enjoy this oasis in the modern world. The smell of sawdust has also flowed from the "woodhick" past to the present.

The Hyde-Murphy Company closed in 1961 but is still in the air. Today, the smell of sawdust permeates Ridgway's air just as when Hyde-Murphy was cutting wood. In 2000, Ridgway started a Chainsaw Carvers Rendezvous, which grew to become the premier event on the town's calendar. Carvers from around the world come to Ridgway to practice their craft. They inherited the mantle of the woodworkers' art from Hyde-Murphy's artisans. New smells came to Ridgway. Now, the smell of sawdust mingles with chainsaw oil, gasoline, and the aroma of festival food on the streets of the town. Saws still create art, just as in the old days of decorative woodworking.

When you walk the streets of Ridgway today, shopping for antiques, on an architectural tour, enjoying a festival, or visiting history, you will be struck by your senses. From Main Street, you can look over the distinctive styling and alluring ornamentation of the storefronts and still see the mountains, which are again covered with the wood that made Ridgway. New-growth forests have replaced the original timber that was turned into functional beauty. You can hear birds sing from the forested hillsides surrounding Ridgway. You can smell festival food roasting and visit local bistros; you can taste ice cream from sidewalk cafes and feel history all around you. The Elk County Highlands are a living organism. Life has flowed out to enrich the world, and new life has flowed back in to invigorate the community. Life changes and renews. Today, in Ridgway, the view is holistic. Forested hillsides brush cloud-speckled skies, and you can watch the river flow or ride on the scenery. The lumber left and returned, and the forest and the people remained. Most importantly, you can experience the air of small-town American life and liberty and pursue happiness.

One

Wood

Ridgway was originally surrounded by thick forests. It was said that when the first tree was cut down, it would not fall because it was supported by surrounding trees. Here, a man with a simple double-bitted ax begins the task of wresting a community and life from the primeval forest; his resolve shines from his face. No task seems too large. (SM.)

What can a man (or boy) with an ax and saw plus co-workers accomplish? They eventually clear-cut Pennsylvania. Fortunes came out of these forests. Towns flourished, and generations succeeded. Most of the fortune never trickled down to these woodhicks, but they were the backbone of the industry. They were on the cutting edge of the ax or saw. (SM.)

Hemlock bark has tannins used to tan animal hides into leather. Eventually, bark became more valuable than wood, and trees were left to rot in the forest after the bark was harvested. It was cheaper to transport buffalo hides from the West than to send the perishable bark there, and Pennsylvania became a center of the tanning industry. Ridgway had three tanneries that contributed to the rise of the local economy. (SM.)

Two woodhicks display the use of a peavey to move logs. A peavey is a pole with a point on the end and a hook on a swivel. Since logs are round, they can be easily rolled to position them for a horse to drag. Horses were the first heavy haulers (after human muscle) to begin the clearing before roads. (SM.)

Teams of horses line up to drag logs. These horses must be proud of their jewelry. They are outfitted like equine gladiators of the forest. Each of the three men in the background holds peaveys to roll logs to be hooked to the horses. The woodhick outfit is standard: long johns, suspenders, loose-fitting pants, heavy work boots, and crush hat. (SM.)

This wintertime scene shows how useful horse teams could be and how they could haul heavy loads through the winter woods. In the background are a large log pile and another team of horses dragging another large load of logs. Shifting logs in the winter was essential, and foot injuries were common. (SM.)

This is clear-cutting. In the last decades of the 19th century and first decades of the 20th century, Pennsylvania was clear cut by lumber barons. Today, there is a second-growth forest, which is managed more sensibly. Imagine the task of the lone teamster with one team of horses looking at this hillside. He may look intimidated, but history shows forests were cleared, and lumbermen moved on. (EC.)

A cruiser was a surveyor who walked through a prospective purchase of new timber and measured trees by their diameter at breast height to estimate the value of the woodlot. He trailed a chain, a thin metal measure that calculated distance. Hopefully, when the wood was cut, his estimate was accurate. This man appears to be surveying a tornado blowdown, but it is actually a recent harvest. (SM.)

A scaler measured how much wood would come out of a stand of timber for prospective buyers. Saw logs were usually measured in 16-foot sections. Another measure was how many board feet or cordwood could be harvested. This elderly timber surveyor stands with his trusty walking stick next to a harvest that hopefully met his estimate. The logs have arrived at a rail landing. (SM.)

This type of collection of logs was known as a "rough and tumble." The etymology of the phrase seems obvious. Sorting out this pile of chaos was the everyday job of the logger. Note the small figure of a lumberjack at the upper right on the pile of logs. He should be very careful not to "tumble." (SM.)

These woodhicks do not seem overly concerned that a log weighing close to a ton is hanging over their heads. They are supremely confident in the technology of the times. Accidents in the woods and on the railways were common; the danger was an accepted part of the job in the big woods. Hard hats and steel-toed boots were a fantasy of the future. (EC.)

Seen here is a very large lumbering operation. This is called a landing, probably beside a watercourse or sawmill. Logs were transported downriver to sawmills. Note the large number of horse teams and the system of log stacking on cross logs for ease of movement. Rough horse paths led down to the landing. (SM.)

An early sawmill uses the water barrel system to catch rainwater for fire suppression. A narrow-gauge rail trestle delivers material to the mill. Several children are visiting, and horses are at the ready. Note the roof ladder to the rain barrels. Sawmills were surrounded by unused slab wood, chips, and sawdust. It was never cleared because when the surrounding timber was cut, the mill was simply moved. (SM.)

Lumber camps were minimalist in design. This camp had a single window, a luxury not all camps enjoyed. The camp was basically just for feeding and sleeping. No frills were needed. After a camp cut the available timber, the camp was taken apart and moved to the new source of wood. How must life have been for the babe-in-arms little girl at right? (SM.)

This camp must have been somewhat gloomy inside. A lonely window cut into the plain board frame as an afterthought reflects the drab lifestyle. Four women of various ages are pictured. Wooden walkways helped them avoid the mud. Note that a woodhick is pouring a friend a libation from a jug in the foreground. "Corn from a jar" was often banned but sometimes flaunted. (SM.)

Frank McChesney's lumber camp on Big Mill Creek was a typical operation. The camp was designed to process large amounts of timber at minimal expense. Crude log huts and bridges set amid the product from start to finish are evident. Note the scattered tree stumps in the foreground and the large log pile in the background. Two woodhicks survey the scene in the distance at center. (EC.)

Woodhicks rarely took breaks, but when they did, there was always a place to sit. Felled logs were everywhere. When it came time to enjoy a pipe or cigar and sit for a commemorative photograph, the men sat amidst a labyrinth of stumps and logs. Music hath charms to soothe these hardy ax wielders. (SM.)

This gang of woodhicks was evidently warned against smiling for their portrait. They hold the tools of their trade: peaveys, a crosscut saw, an oil can, and a sawmill blade. The roof boards are not even trimmed because it was extra work on a building that was only temporary. They look like they have just finished a hard day in the woods. (SM.)

Alcohol was often banned at lumber camps, although at this camp, two men seem to be enjoying a beverage. Tobacco was a highly prized necessity. One man here enjoys a pipe while another is pulling a chaw. Music was a comfort for all genders and ages. A man handy with a squeezebox was a valuable member of the camp. The sweet sound of "Amazing Grace" and jug lightning enlivened many a long night at lumber camp. Note the outhouse in the background. (SM.)

Two

WATER

Water is essential to life. Ridgway is at the confluence of Elk Creek and the Clarion River. Notice the conditions of roads here on Elk Creek. Water was needed for the transportation of the area's resources to market. The infrastructure of roads and rivers was essential to economic growth before Ridgway could develop its potential. (EC.)

This is a view of the Clarion River in Ridgway from the Main Street bridge. The Clarion River has been designated a national wild and scenic river. Hillsides were deforested, but today have regained their forest cloak. This is the waterway that Ridgway used to deliver logs downstream to sawmills. (MW.)

Here is an example of one of the many splash dams that were constructed throughout Elk County by the timbering industry to facilitate the transportation of logs downstream. When all of the small dams were released, or dynamited in some cases, the resulting flood moved logs along to downriver sawmills to be cut into boards. The log driving season was in early spring. (EC.)

The first thing a sawmill needed was a millpond. Railroads delivered logs to a millpond next to the sawmill. Ponds were needed to store logs before cutting and for moving logs into the mill. This example is Byron Ely's sawmill on Elk Creek in Ridgway. Ely came to Ridgway in 1836 and continued lumbering into the 20th century. (EC.)

Here is a landing on a watercourse. Before railroads, logs were delivered to landings for floating individual logs downriver to sawmills. Logs were marked with separate brands to prevent theft and sent downriver. And yes, there were log rustlers who attempted to steal logs. Later, log rafts were used, and finally, the logs were sawn locally. Whether this is a log drive or sawmill pond is unknown. (SM.)

This millpond is at the Hyde and Thayer lumbering operation at Laurel Mill, just west of Ridgway. Logs are being stored prior to being sawed. The sawmill has a small community growing around it. Sawmills employed enough workers to create a village. The site today is the Sandy Beach Recreation Area of Ridgway. (EC.)

Log driving and log rafting could not be practiced on the same waterway. Some streams used one method and some the other. Fighting between practitioners of the two methods was fierce before rafting won out. This scene is from Spring Creek in Elk County. Railroads ended the era of log driving and rafting. A railroad is seen along the creek here. (EC.)

Lumber rafts were built upside down on the bank and then flipped into the river. This scene is along the Clarion River at Belltown. Rafts were floated downriver and then taken apart, with the men walking back upriver. Ridgway sent log rafts via the Clarion and Allegheny Rivers downstream to sawmills as far as Pittsburgh and New Orleans. (EC.)

Rafts were floated down the river right after ice-out in the spring. The water was very cold and dangerous. A "snubber" was a man who waded or swam ashore with a rope to wrap around a tree to stop the huge raft. The snubber had to avoid getting his hands inside the rope when the raft slammed to a halt for the night. Hypothermia was an occupational hazard. (EC.)

This scene is from Cooksburg on the Clarion River. Many rafts are ready to go downriver. One has a shanty built on it for the raftsmen. The shanty held a cooking kitchen and bunks for resting at night. The Cook family lumbering operation was large, and the area is today Cook Forest State Park. (SM.)

Here is another scene from Cooksburg on the Clarion River. The size of these rafts was truly amazing. Log rafts were heavy, large, and unwieldy. They almost filled the river and were very hard to pilot. The amount of lumber shown here is impressive. Lumber baron Andrew Cook's home is at left. (SM.)

As log rafting increased, arks were built as auxiliary support craft. These rafts were (from left to right) a cooking/dining and laundry ark, sleeping quarters, and a floating barn for draft horses. Note the washing tubs hanging on the first ark. This colorful era ended when local sawmills flourished and railroads moved the lumber to market. (SM.)

Logging rafts continue to be built for historical and ceremonial purposes. This raft, shown in Clearfield, Pennsylvania, was constructed for the bicentennial of the county. It was built to historical dimensions with historical tools and techniques. The author is shown on the raft that his students at Penn State DuBois built and subsequently piloted down Clearfield Creek and the Susquehanna River for a short distance. (Debra McGeehan.)

The author, a history professor at Penn State DuBois and Pitt Bradford, is shown at the tiller of the Clearfield bicentennial logging raft built by his students. A typical raft was 70 feet long and 15 feet wide. It weighed 20 tons and contained 5,000 board feet of lumber. Each of the two (fore and aft) tillers was 17 feet long, making the total length of the raft 105 feet. (Debra McGeehan.)

When the raft was on the river, it did not get sideways. The length of the craft would have reached from bank to bank in narrow sections. It took a great deal of engineering to float a raft down the river to market. Rapids, snags, eddies, and low water were constant hurdles. The extremely cold water was a constant threat to success and actual life on the voyage down the river. (Dennis McGeehan.)

Three

Rail

The Barnhart Loader revolutionized timber transport. The loader would lift a flatcar from behind it, place it behind the locomotive, load it with logs, and then proceed to the next flatcar behind it. This allowed timber removal from the steep, narrow valleys of north-central Pennsylvania. Log trains could deliver to local sawmills. (SM.)

Logs were removed from the narrow valleys of Pennsylvania by narrow-gauge railroads. These railroads were temporary, and their faint trails can be seen everywhere in the woods today. They were not always arrow-straight, as can be seen in this example. Before the invention of the Barnhart loader, dual tracks were needed to manage large log piles in narrow spaces. (SM.)

When the log train arrived at the millpond landing, the logs were unloaded. Often, the logs had become stuck or frozen. A man with a pry bar had to get on top of the load and loosen the logs without being carried into the ensuing discharge. Logs splashing into the millpond were an impressive sight. (SM.)

These men, either railroad workers or woodhicks, are hitching a ride on a loaded log train. This scene looks incredibly dangerous, although the men seem unperturbed. It seems they put a lot of faith in the logs remaining in place and not shifting. Hard hats had not been imagined yet. Safety was an individual responsibility. (SM.)

This is the Pennsylvania Railroad station in Ridgway prior to 1907. Steam is issuing from the train, horses are waiting to transport passengers, and a man is casually strolling past the old wooden station down North Broad Street, a shotgun over his shoulder. This original wooden station was replaced by a brick structure built by the Hyde-Murphy Company. (EC.)

The Hyde-Murphy Company built this beautiful redbrick Pennsylvania Railroad passenger station in 1907 on North Broad Street. In this view, a number of residents are waiting. Waiting for arrivals or departures of the dominant mode of transport at that time was common. Several trains per day moved through Ridgway and prided themselves on punctuality. (EC.)

The Pennsylvania Railroad station on North Broad Street in Ridgway was unused, closed, and in shabby condition for many years. The tracks were still being used, but not the station. It was feared that the old architectural gem might be lost. A part of Ridgway's heritage was in danger, and action from concerned citizenry was needed. (Dennis McGeehan.)

The citizens of Ridgway rose to the challenge. After years of decline, the station has been restored to its former elegance. It now commands a site on the banks of Elk Creek on North Broad Street. The beautiful redbrick structure shines beside tracks that are today little used. New uses for old buildings save significant historical architecture. (Dennis McGeehan.)

Time has passed this Pennsylvania Railroad station by like a ghost locomotive living in the memories of old train buffs. In the imagination, whistles scream, people bustle, and cargoes trundle. Wood smoke lingers in the air, and steam billows. Civilized nations should not lose their history. Some teach history, but all are taught by history. (Dennis McGeehan.)

A car passes by the Pennsylvania Railroad station on North Broad Street in Ridgway. The automobile is the reason that the railroad station has become a footnote to the past. Modern transportation has gone down different paths than past routes. Today, Americans are very mobile and not confined to the steel rails of the past. A constant here is hills full of trees. (Dennis McGeehan.)

This scene is a collage of Ridgway's and America's transportation history. Water was used first by pioneers forging into the frontier. Roads followed and improved over the years. Railroads crisscrossed the county. Two separate rail lines diverge here. Modern highways and bridges gave Americans the mobility they cherished. Finally, the preservation of historic transportation structures like train stations was accomplished. (Dennis McGeehan.)

The Buffalo, Rochester & Pittsburgh Railroad eventually became the Baltimore & Ohio Railroad. Its passenger station on West Main Street in Ridgway was a redbrick structure with sloping gabled dormers and multiple quoins. This building was also erected by the Hyde-Murphy Company. No longer in service as a railroad station, the building has had several tenants in recent years. (MW.)

Today, the old Baltimore & Ohio Railroad Station has been restored but is still unoccupied. The building is a beautiful architectural treasure. Its numerous, large white stone quoins and red brick finish give the building a kind of jigsaw exterior that makes it stand out as visually exciting. (Dennis McGeehan.)

A Palladian-style window triptych decorates the side of the Pennsylvania Railroad station in Ridgway below its date stone, 1907. The building is badly in need of repairs. Bricks are fading, wood is aging, and roof tiles need to be replaced. It is apparent that the Hyde-Murphy Company paid homage to historic architectural styles when constructing this edifice. (Dennis McGeehan.)

Today, beautifully restored, the Pennsylvania Railroad station gleams in the sunlight and sparkles along North Broad Street. The building proclaims the name of the stop, as all railroad stations do. It includes a dormer with elegant windows and a wooden keystone-shaped keystone. The building also has a beautiful dentiled cornice that creates dynamic shadowing. (Dennis McGeehan.)

Four

Sawmills

Ridgway is in the Lumber Heritage Region of Pennsylvania. The Lumber Museum in Potter County has a restored sawmill and lumber camp. It is a modern place to experience what lumber history was like. Local sawmills sprang up to process the timber without having to transport it miles downriver. Local economies boomed. Joseph Smith Hyde started a sawmill in Ridgway and became the leading lumberman of Elk County. (Dennis McGeehan.)

Sawmills sprang up everywhere in north-central Pennsylvania. Shay locomotives on narrow-gauge railroads delivered logs to millponds. Sawmill workers wore spike-soled boots and ran across the surface of the logs and maneuvered them up the loading ramp into the sawmill. They carried a trusty balance bar and used it to push logs along. Logrolling was a specialized skill that the men became proficient at. (SM.)

The Lumber Museum holds an annual Barkpeelers Convention, and Cherry Springs State Park hosts the Woodsmen's Carnival, where modern woodhicks practice traditional skills like log rolling and compete for prizes. Logrolling is a special skill that sawmill workers prized and that helped prevent foot injuries. Evidently, being a man was never essential to being a skilled logroller. (Dennis McGeehan.)

At the annual Cherry Springs State Park Woodsmen's Carnival, current lumberjacks compete for prizes. Wood harvesting is still a thriving part of the Pennsylvania economy, and planned selective forest cutting preserves Penn's Woods. These modern workers try to best each other in front of large audiences. (The lumberjack on the left won this one.) (Dennis McGeehan.)

The locomotives have delivered so many logs that the rails are not even visible. Cross logs have been set up to store logs and keep them loose for when they are ready to go into the mill. Buildings were in some places crude and temporary. This storage yard looks extremely jumbled and makeshift. (SM.)

The Lumber Museum in Potter County has a restored sawmill, millpond, museum, and train shed with a locomotive. On the Fourth of July, it holds a Barkpeelers Convention, including woodhick games and events. The lumber heritage of Pennsylvania survives in this corner of the state. (Dennis McGeehan.)

The interior of a sawmill is pictured. These sites created hundreds of jobs and lifetimes of work for residents of the forest communities. It looks like a cluttered workplace, and it was a time before safety regulations were created. Workers were responsible for their own safety, and accidents were common. The saw blade is about halfway through cutting a board off of this log. (SM.)

The sawmill at Hallton built large and long trestles to hold the finished lumber from the mill. The trestle stretched along the Clarion River. Today, this river has been designated a national wild and scenic river, and the waterway is plied by recreational watercraft. Canoeists marvel at the scenic beauty of the Clarion and conjure up visions of historical scenes like this. (EC.)

The Eagle Valley Tannery's splash dam in Ridgway resulted in much debris in the river. Pennsylvania had 870 tanneries in 1870. In 1900, the state led the nation in leather production. Tanneries made sole leather, clothing, engine belts, and horse harnesses. Large tanneries could process 600,000 hides annually, using 50,000 cords of hemlock bark and logging 5,000 acres a year. Buffalo hides from the American West were shipped here for processing. (EC.)

Joseph S. Hyde came to Ridgway in 1837, working for Enos Gillis. He left to work in the woods in Wisconsin. He returned to Ridgway and married Jane Gillis, his former employer's daughter. She was also the niece of James Lyle Gillis, who was the land manager for town founder Jacob Ridgway. He began working in sawmills and purchasing timberlands until he was the leading lumberman in the area. (EC.)

Walter P. Murphy operated a planing mill in Freeport, Armstrong County. His lumber was supplied by J.S. Hyde & Son of Ridgway. Murphy eventually came to Ridgway to co-found the Hyde-Murphy Company in 1884 with Joseph Smith Hyde. The firm established offices in Pittsburgh, Philadelphia, New York, and Washington, DC, becoming a leading supplier of high-quality architectural woodwork. The partnership was uniquely successful and long-lasting. (EC.)

Five

PARTNERSHIP

This drawing of the Hyde-Murphy Company depicts the many buildings that made up the complex. These include the main factory, the engine house, the office, the door & sash warehouse, the dry kiln building, the lumber shed, the shipping department, the screen door department, the glue department, the frame department, a barn, and several warehouses. At the bottom, a large lumber yard is depicted. (EC.)

Henry Clay Park was the resident architect for the Hyde-Murphy Company. He was born in Waverly, New York, and began his career as an architect in Punxsutawney, Jefferson County, in 1891. He moved to Ridgway in 1894, becoming a very busy designer of significant buildings and interiors. He designed the Ridgway Hospital and High School and many of the Lilies of the Valley mansions in Ridgway. (EC)

As the Hyde family influence declined in the company, Walter Murphy's influence increased. His creative genius at business and innovation in developing new processes in wood milling made the company famous around the country. The business burned in 1910 but reopened in new buildings within two years. Walter was succeeded as general manager by his son Samuel. The company eventually closed in 1961 after creating architectural history. (EC.)

This is an early view of the Hyde-Murphy Company at North Mill and Race Streets in Ridgway. Workers are posed for a portrait. A horse-drawn wagon is exiting the mill. Overhead cranes and a conveyor track for moving freight are visible. Many of Ridgway's historic homes came out of this building. (EC.)

This is a later view of the same scene as the previous image. An extension has been added to the left side of the building, and more workers are evident in doors and windows. There are also now three wagons in view. Lumber is moving in and out of the mill. (EC.)

In an even later view, the mill has grown even larger. The addition seen in the last image has been expanded again and now seems to surround the original section of the mill. This is still in the horse-drawn carriage era. The workers take a break to document the business. (EC.)

After another round of expansions, the Hyde-Murphy Company main building looked like this. The building announced that the company provided general contracting and the manufacture of buildings, hardwood mantels, stair work, grills, veneered doors, plate windows, and art glass. The building features a clerestory, an elevated section of wall that includes windows for light, fresh air, or both. (EC.)

The Hyde-Murphy Planing Mill was at Race Street and North Mill Avenue. It was a brick building that was built after the devastating fire of 1910 that leveled the business. Horse-drawn delivery wagons were still in use at this time, and it appears that a school group is in the process of getting a tour of the building. (MW.)

This ivy-covered building at the corner of Race and Mill Streets was the former Hyde-Murphy Company factory. It was operational until 1961 and was torn down in 1974. The site is now occupied by the Lyle G. Hall Community Park. The complex of Hyde-Murphy buildings covered a sizable area just north of Main Street in Ridgway. (EC.)

At one time, the Hyde-Murphy Company employed over 300 workers in 15 different buildings. In this view, a group of workers takes a break to pose for a photograph. Some of them have posed reclining on the roof. Note that rail systems were used to convey materials around the complex. Wood was the product, and the company's buildings were made of wood before the great fire of 1910. (EC.)

In this photograph of the interior of the Hyde-Murphy Company, it is apparent why factory buildings had clerestories. Single overhead lightbulbs are the only artificial light. The infusion of natural light coming in the clerestory was essential for illumination. The workers are putting together doors on ever-present sawhorses. A profusion of hand tools, vices, planers, paint, and glue cans is visible along the assembly line. (EC.)

This interior view of the Hyde-Murphy Company door and sash department finds workers posed for a photograph. Work in progress is visible on sawhorses, while finished products lean against the walls. Vices mounted on workbenches and wood planers are part of the artists' tools. The mustache seemed to be a popular look at the time. (EC.)

This scene is also inside the door and sash department of the mill. Many completed works are lying on sawhorses, ready for further finishing. They are awaiting door panels or mullions depending on whether they will be turned into doors or windows. Assembly line production was used at this facility. (EC.)

Inside the Hyde-Murphy Company mill finishing department, workers are making wood finishing products for architectural use. Windows, door frame arches, and pediments are in evidence. Note the heading on the wide door frame. The Hyde-Murphy Company was famous for elegant decorative woodwork that is still extant in many homes in Ridgway. (EC.)

This is the glue shop inside the Hyde-Murphy Company, where panels were glued up into plywood and veneers. The worker on the left is Sam Frederico, with his son Jimmy in the middle. The man on the right is unidentified. Custom veneers were a specialty of the Hyde-Murphy Company. (EC.)

Here is an interior photograph from the Hyde-Murphy Company. Milling lathes are seen at right, and above the floor, stored above, are spare band saws. Workbenches are on the left. It is apparent how complicated and specialized the machinery was. These workers were highly competent at using state-of-the-art devices. Sawhorses seem to have been a standard low-tech tool. (EC.)

The horse-drawn era is now over, and the Hyde-Murphy Company lumber truck is now motorized. It looks like finished millwork is being delivered to a building site by the company truck. Hopefully, the distance from the mill is not too far, as two workers are assigned to hold the load in place for delivery. Modern workplace safety procedures would preclude this kind of practice today. (EC.)

Here is a group portrait of the Murphy family and employees. From left to right are Hyde-Murphy Company co-founder Walter P. Murphy, L. Klingel, Joe Drennen, Albert Bright, Ray Krape, Mary Redding, Samuel Murphy, and Chas. Kline. Samuel was the son of Walter Murphy. The photograph was taken on June 28, 1903. (EC.)

Joseph Smith Hyde was born in Tamworth, Carroll County, New Hampshire on August 30, 1813, and died in Ridgway on June 30, 1888. He is buried in the Evergreen Cemetery in Painesville, Ohio. The Hyde family mausoleum is in the Ridgway Cemetery and is constructed of cut stone, including a small entrance stairway. It is Classical in design, with Corinthian columns supporting an entablature that includes a pediment with a decorative carving. (EC).

Six

Community

Lumber yards were a common sight in Ridgway. Byron Ely's lumber yard is seen here. The bridge at lower left crosses Elk Creek on Depot Street. The large white building at right-center is Hyde's Department Store on Main Street. To the right of that is the original Elk County Courthouse. This is one of only two photographs of that building known to exist. (EC.)

The first Elk County Courthouse in Ridgway was built in 1845 by Edward H. Derby of wood frame construction. A white picket fence between stone columns fronted it. A church steeple is visible behind the courthouse to the right. The first courthouse lasted for 34 years before being replaced in 1879. (EC.)

The second and present Elk County Courthouse was built in 1879 by J.P. Marston. It was built of red brick and dressed white sandstone. It was built in the Second Empire style, with a mansard roof, bell tower, and nine-foot diameter clock on all four faces. The building was originally surmounted by a nine-foot zinc statue of Justice, which was struck by lightning and removed. (Dennis McGeehan.)

This view of Ridgway was taken from the east on Boot Jack Hill. Hall Dam is in the foreground. Ridgway spreads out to the left, or west. The Elk County Courthouse tower is visible at left. To the right of that is the Hyde-Murphy Company. A water tank of the facility is visible, and several active smokestacks to the right show the company was busy at this time. (EC.)

In this view of Ridgway, the Buffalo, Rochester & Pittsburgh Railroad crosses just below the town. At the lower edge of town, the Hyde-Murphy Company sits along Elk Creek. Above that, on Main Street, the Elk County Courthouse is visible. In the background, the dirt road snaking up Boot Jack Hill can be seen. (EC.)

Here is a view of Ridgway from the west with the hill behind the courthouse in the background. The Elk County Courthouse is visible at center left. The Hyde-Murphy Company buildings are at bottom left, just above the copse of trees. The hill behind the courthouse in the background is mostly fields in this view; today, it is forested. (EC.)

This view of Ridgway is looking north up the Clarion River Valley. The Elk County Courthouse is at center right. The Hyde-Murphy Company buildings are just above the large white building at center, which is the Masonic Temple. Several active smokestacks of the Hyde-Murphy Company can be seen in the background. (EC.)

This aerial view of Ridgway looks northeast. Main Street runs diagonally from bottom left to top right. One block north, or left, of Main Street is the Hyde-Murphy Company. The company's water tank is visible, surrounded by the company's other buildings. (EC.)

This is a later view of downtown Ridgway from the same angle. The Elk County Courthouse is at right, toward the top. The Hyde-Murphy Company water tank is now gone, but the rest of the complex's buildings are visible in the outfield of the baseball diamond at top left. Elk Creek is at far left. (EC.)

This view of Ridgway was taken from the west. Elk Creek Valley is at top, and the Clarion River Valley is to the left. The Dickinson bridge over the Clarion River is the white bridge at center. The Hyde-Murphy Company buildings are above and just left of the bridge. Smoke is coming from the factory, and the water tank is still in place. (EC.)

Here is a view of Ridgway from the north. The buildings of the Hyde-Murphy complex can be seen at left, with the water tank above. To the right of that is the Elk County Courthouse and the large white Masonic Temple. The large building at far right is the Ridgway Hospital. Today, forests have reclaimed the hill seen to the south here. (EC.)

Eventually, the original Hyde Department Store became the Hall, Kaul & Hyde Department Store, the largest of its kind in western Pennsylvania. Here, the store is decorated with patriotic flags and bunting, possibly for the Fourth of July. Ridgway held parades for Independence Day on Main Street past stores decorated for the occasion. Later, this became the Smith Brothers Department Store. (EC.)

The Hyde Hotel was at the corner of Main and Broad Streets. It was a five-story structure with wrap-around balconies on three of the floors. It was the elite place to stay for visitors to Ridgway. Horse-drawn carriages ply their trade as well-dressed gentlemen stroll the streets. (EC.)

This is the intersection of Main (left to right) and North Broad Streets in Ridgway during the second decade of the 20th century. Only one early iron horse can be seen, and it seems to be drawing curious looks from pedestrians. Note the water trough at lower left. Real horses still trotted through town. (MW.)

The Hyde Hotel has moved into the automobile age in the early decades of the 20th century. The multi-chromatic exterior is evident here, with a white cornice and white balconies accenting the redbrick walls. There is a lunch counter in the building on the North Broad Street side. (MW.)

In the 1930s, the automobile styles have changed. The hotel has added more fire escapes, and there is now a Western Union office on the North Broad Street side. Note the traffic light mounted on a platform in the middle of the intersection. The hotel looks busy from the number of cars parked outside. (EC.)

The influence of the Hyde-Murphy Company was usually evident in Ridgway. In this scene from the 1913 Fourth of July parade, the company water tank is a conspicuous, ever-present symbol towering over the town. It was an era of straw hats and the beginning of the automobile age. (EC.)

The Elk County National Bank sits at the main intersection in Ridgway at Main and Broad Streets. The bank was founded in 1874 by Jerome Powell, and this ornate structure in the Neoclassical style was built by the Hyde-Murphy Company in 1889. Over the years, the building hosted a radio station, a sporting goods store, a senior center, a dance studio, a jewelry shop, and a restaurant. (EC.)

In the 1940s, Elk County National Bank's clean architectural lines and décor grace Main Street. The building includes an ornate overhanging cornice with dentils and brackets. The building on the left, on Main Street, is the Smith Brothers Department Store. It connected through the back with its other building on the right on North Broad Street. (EC.)

For many years, the Elk County National Bank was unoccupied. It was restored to its former glory and is today the home of a craft brewery and restaurant. The building is constructed of redbrick decorated with grey trim. The cornice is especially ornate and strikingly grand. The multiple windows lend a beautiful symmetry to the building. (Dennis McGeehan.)

The front of the bank is not wide, but it makes up for it in complexity. The Classical doorway is within another Classical-style front. Both include pilasters. The pediment of the doorway is surmounted by a cartouche-style heading. The pediments of the front element support an entablature with a frieze of circular bullseyes. The cornice of the frontage is overlooked by carved lion heads. (Dennis McGeehan.)

The Elk County National Bank building is today the Brew Bank Brewing Company. The craft brewery includes a restaurant that incorporates the old bank lobby, a beautiful example of the Hyde-Murphy Company's elegant work. The marble, mahogany, and intricate woodwork are a reminder of the opulence of early-20th-century banking. Large safes are still reminiscent of the security provided by these institutions. (EC.)

The Brew Bank serves craft beer and food in a unique historic setting. A large safe from the old bank sits behind the bar and accents the period décor. It is a wonderful example of the reuse of historic old facilities for new uses. Set at the main intersection of Ridgway, across from the courthouse, it is a perfect gathering place for the county seat. (Dennis McGeehan.)

One can sit at the bar and watch beer being made and then drink it. Lifting their eyes as they lift a stein, customers can look out the window and see the beautiful architecture of the town, including the historic county courthouse. Slightly higher are the forest-clad hills that are again tree-covered with the wood that enriched this town. If it is Rendezvous Week, visitors can see the wood being made into art. (Dennis McGeehan.)

This complicated walk-in vault was part of the Elk County National Bank. Safe deposit boxes can be seen inside. These safes were intended to portray safety and security; however, they also exhibited a sign of the times. Victorian decoration and ornamentation were part of the obsession with artistic display of the times. Today, it is a delightful vision of a historical time and business. (EC.)

The very beautiful, polished walk-in vault has been preserved and today serves as a beer cooler, probably the fanciest and most secure beer in the world. The machinery of the vault door is visible and offers an amazing view of the complex safeguards of old banks. Polished brass and glass create a powerful vision. (Dennis McGeehan.)

The step from the floor into the vault is another reminder of Ridgway's past. Northcentral Pennsylvania had sizeable deposits of clay, and brickworks were common throughout the area. Ridgway had a brickworks, and companies often stamped their products with their name. Today, some people collect bricks from historic foundries. (Dennis McGeehan.)

This is the main intersection of Ridgway and shows the influence of the Hyde-Murphy Company. On the right is the Hyde Department Store. On the left is the Hyde House Hotel (with balconies) and beside it is the Elk County National Bank (building with awnings to right) with Hyde-Murphy millwork inside. The street is being repaired under the watchful eyes of idle children, while a disinterested stroller and a dog pass by. (EC.)

The Ridgway YMCA is an important center of community life. Over the years, it has held classes, lectures, theatrical and musical performances, and features a gymnasium and swimming pool. The building was constructed of sand-colored brick by the Hyde-Murphy Company. It includes three extended porticoes, two entrance porticoes, and a window extension. (Dennis McGeehan.)

The Armory Building was erected by the Hyde-Murphy Company in red brick. It is a plain building with a Romanesque arch on plain pilasters. The facade is a simple rectangular triptych with no ornamentation on the cornice. Even the windows are unadorned. The window sills and base course are the only exception and are of plain masonry. (Dennis McGeehan.)

This is the Elk County General Hospital, which is part of the Penn Highlands Health Center today. It was built in 1901 and designed by Henry C. Park, resident architect of the Hyde-Murphy Company. The company erected many different kinds of buildings in Ridgway and around the country. Note the solarium rooms on both floors at both ends of this Neoclassical building. (EC.)

The Hyde-Murphy Company built many churches, including one in Honolulu, Hawaii. This example is the First Baptist Church on Mill Street in Ridgway. The Gothic Revival–style building served two separate congregations, Baptist and Christian Missionary Alliance. The building has been a private home and is today a doctor's office. (Dennis McGeehan.)

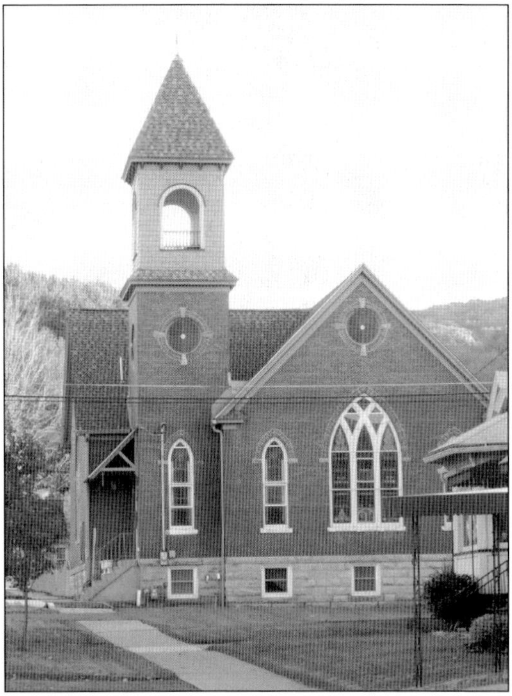

Buildings are functional art, and architecture and art flourish in historic Ridgway. This factory building displays a mural of Clarion River history, including canoeing Native Americans and historic log rafters. Modern canoeists on the Clarion River are not represented, but one can see them in real time behind this building on most seasonal days. Buildings became the palette for expression that keeps history and art in the public's consciousness. (Dennis McGeehan.)

A redbrick garage on Montmorenci Road just outside of Ridgway became a work of art as an amateur Van Gogh created a version of *Starry Night* that lasts all day and winter. Art remembers history. It strives and yearns to interpret life. When life is understandable, communities knit together and flourish. Art comforts and celebrates. Ridgway is a welcoming home to art. (Dennis McGeehan.)

Take a walk through Ridgway. Look out and look up. The eyes are the windows to the soul. Look in. Is someone looking back? Look back at art and history, and take a moment to say, "hello in there," as John Prine wrote. Storefronts are gaudy works of architectural artwork. Art and history mirror Ridgway's past from many secret nooks and crannies. If one just looks, they will find their own private secret garden in the machine. (Dennis McGeehan.)

Shakespeare wrote, "But soft, what light through yonder window breaks?" Ridgway is romantic. Maybe a Juliet (or Romeo) is secretly watching and wondering behind one of these windows. Ridgway is full of possibilities and initiative for the future. Behind the vacant windows lurk redevelopment and progress. Stay tuned—new windows and doors are opening. Stairways and progress are looking up. (Dennis McGeehan.)

The Hyde-Murphy Company was active throughout Elk County. It built the Johnsonburg Community Center at the main intersection downtown. It has been the center of community life in Johnsonburg since 1921. The paper mill, seen here at left, built the facility for the residents. This scene is from the grand opening celebration in 1921. Almost everyone in town attended. (EC.)

The Johnsonburg Community Center was built by the Hyde-Murphy Company in 1921 for the New York and Pennsylvania Company paper pill and presented to the community. It has served as municipal offices, a library, and meeting rooms. It had a swimming pool, basketball court, and outdoor playground. The brick building was constructed in the Neoclassical style. (Dennis McGeehan.)

The Harry Stackpole residence on North Michael Street in St. Marys was constructed by the Hyde-Murphy Company of cut stone. Today, it is the Lynch-Green Funeral Home. It had a large wrap-around porch with simple Doric columns and three large dormers. The second story features several bay windows. The entrance portico is a colonnaded porch. (Dennis McGeehan.)

Harry Stackpole founded the Stackpole Carbon Company, once the largest employer in Elk County. This was his first residence. For many years, it was the John J. Lynch Funeral Home; today, it is the Lynch-Green Funeral Home. The beautiful mansion is close to the St. Marys downtown. The three levels feature columns, bays, and dormers, with a Palladian-style window in the end gable. (Dennis McGeehan.)

Harry Stackpole's second residence at the end of Maurus Street was a Hyde-Murphy Company house designed in the Dutch Colonial Revival style. It has a gambrel roof, a flared gable with overhang, dormer double windows, and gable-end chimneys with gable windows. The roof was covered in beautiful pink and grey slates. A front half-porch featured Doric columns. A rear addition with a large chimney almost doubled the size of the mansion. (Dennis McGeehan.)

This rear view of the mansion shows a three-level breezeway connecting the residence to a three-car garage with a second-story apartment with a triple window dormer and attached first-floor tool shed. At far left is an attached glass greenhouse. The structure had two full-size basements with a billiard room, ping-pong table, craft room, and wine cellar. (Dennis McGeehan.)

This view of the recently renovated Stackpole House shows that many of the original windows have been removed, and a new roof has been added. The tool shed is gone. The bay window on the first floor of the main wing at one time had a built-in indoor goldfish pond. The mansion had six bedrooms, six bathrooms, three walk-in cedar closets, eight fireplaces, and untold memories. "Knowledge is made of memory," as Plato wrote. (Dennis McGeehan.)

The Stackpole mansion's rear addition was a knotty pine room that filled the entire first floor. It was paneled with wide pine boards and stained a deep amber shade that glowed with prominent mahogany-colored knots. A wide bay window enclosed a terrarium platform. The room included a library and a bar. Exposed beams made the space truly opulent. (Dennis McGeehan.)

The Stackpole mansion also had an oak-paneled den and a formal dining room with a butler's pantry and dumb waiter. This view is from the bay window room. The bay enclosed an indoor goldfish pond. The room included a decorative poured concrete fireplace with ceramic tiles and a Franklin stove. The ceiling was coffered with moldings surrounding floral patterns. Hyde-Murphy signature designs filled the residence. (Dennis McGeehan.)

The doors and windows of perception may be ornate and distinctive. The Hyde-Murphy Company's elegance and attention to detail are apparent in this view of the three-level breezeway. Decorative crescent moon shutters with window boxes and a rose arbor trellis flanked by sitting benches allow visitors to enjoy the lush flower plantings. A full-time gardener was employed, and a greenhouse kept the flowers seasonal. Note the purple martin house on the roof. (Dennis McGeehan.)

When Harry Stackpole built his cabin in the woods, he sought "the tonic of wildness," in Thoreau's words. The site was outside of town. Today, it is surrounded by a hospital campus, church, convent, monastery, grade school, and high school. His wife built this chapel in the woods behind the mansion. Catholic nuns operated the hospital, and this way station was on their path through the woods between the convent and the hospital. It remains, little visited. (Dennis McGeehan.)

Seven

SMOKE AND WATER

In 1901, Ridgway was a bustling small town with a thriving economy. The main business in town was the Hyde-Murphy Company, a producer of high-quality millwork for the architectural trade. The mill was on Race Street, which was one block behind this scene of Main Street. (EC.)

On April 23, 1910, Ridgway suffered the most devastating fire in its history when the Hyde-Murphy Company went up in flames. The huge blaze consumed most of the company's buildings and burned an entire block from Mill Street to Main Street. The conflagration raged throughout the night, creating this otherworldly scene reminiscent of Dante's *Inferno*. (EC.)

This scene is from 4:00 a.m. on April 23, 1910. This is not sunrise; it is illuminated solely by fire. Some of the walls were still standing, like the skeleton of a great dying beast. The 15-building complex of the Hyde-Murphy Company, mostly made of wood, was quickly consumed. Windows designed to let in light were now a view into the inferno. (EC.)

When the sun came up, the scale of the devastation was apparent. Some walls were still standing, but many were not. The fire burned from Race Street to Main Street, and witnesses knew that their town was changed forever. The ruins smoked for days, and residents came out to witness the historic event's aftermath. (EC.)

The air of Ridgway was filled with smoke, and the smell was in the air for weeks. Some nearby stone or brick structures also burned, and some of their walls stood, but they suffered severe smoke and fire damage. As people ventured out and stood on piles of rubble, it was as if they were witnessing a battlefield. It was a battlefield—between firemen and fire. (EC.)

Here in the background stands the Smith Brothers Company Department Store, which survived the conflagration. Everywhere one looked, there were piles of rubble, and viewers could only speculate on what they were looking at. Random stone piers, upended wheels, and brick structures of unknown use silently smoked away. It was not one building that had burned but a whole neighborhood. A bright spring day was overcast with the haze of disaster. (EC.)

Two lone firemen stand mutely gazing skyward through the rising smoke and fumes of their world, changed forever, wondering what new landscape was the new normal. They must have been resting and recuperating after a night of hectic and heroic struggle against an enemy without logic or purpose. Fire's only impulse is to spread until controlled. Firefighting came first, followed by cleanup, an equally daunting task. (EC.)

Behind the M.M. Store, a wooden building collapsed while a brick building beside it survived. The material that a building was made of was significant in its chances for survival and possible rehabilitation. Ridgway planners' hopes also rose as forward-thinking developers could already see a restored and improved town. (EC.)

In a scene reminiscent of images of World War I battlefields, pools of standing water, smoking potholes, and ruined trees litter the landscape. The almost complete destruction of the business is evident from this photograph. The company decided to rebuild the wooden complex in brick, and it continued in business for another 51 years. (EC.)

In "My City of Ruins," Bruce Springsteen wrote, "Rise up!" Men in suits, probably Hyde-Murphy Company officials, examine the wreckage and plan a route forward. Surviving buildings stand as mute witnesses to their fallen partners. An entire city block was now open and ready for redevelopment. Whatever shade trees the block had were turned into stark, bare poles, like the one on the right. Fire hoses trace the new routes through town. (EC.)

Throngs of the curious came out to see for themselves what had transpired. This scene is from the Elk County Courthouse lawn. Across the street, some buildings were gutted, and some still stood. Windows that were filled yesterday with merchandise now were like blinded eyes staring back at shocked residents. A new vision was needed to guide the town to new horizons. (EC.)

Everyone in Ridgway who lived through the great fire measured their life relative to it. Young and old told and retold stories of what they were doing and what they saw. Here, two sets of residents survey the damage side by side. Two young boys, possibly brothers, stand on rubble while two men in suits and bowlers do the exact same thing nearby. (EC.)

Like Dickens's tale, here is the ghost of Ridgway, past, present, and future. The present is represented by the skeletons of former buildings and businesses. The past is gone. Ridgway's future is beginning. Two young boys on scooters will be the future of the town. Youth is ever in motion, and these two boys only slowed down briefly to register as faint images. One gazes at the photographer from the past. (EC.)

After the fire, all levels of Ridgway society came out to see the changes. Old and young, rich and poor, speculated about how the massive change would affect their lives. Here, observing the ruins of their town, residents crowd the streets. Fashions of the time are notable. Gentlemen wore bowlers or derbies. Working men wore the familiar cap of their trade, and youths wore the newsboy-style cap. (EC.)

Ridgway's Main Street was a scene of chaos. Many windows were out. Buildings were missing. Ladders leaned against buildings. Store windows were filled with ruined merchandise and would not open for some time. The building on the left is decorated for a planned parade with patriotic bunting. At that time, most storefronts had canopies to shield them from the sun. The sun would not come out in Ridgway for a time. (EC.)

This is the area of Main Street where the fire burned through. The building on the right was saved, and buildings on the left were saved. The area in the middle is the section where buildings had to be razed and rebuilt. Obviously, business and traffic in Ridgway were disrupted for some time. Crowds of rubberneckers are still milling about. (EC.)

In the background, horse-drawn firefighting equipment is busy, surrounded by firemen. In the foreground, children marvel at the busy scene. Fire, horse wagons, and general high anxiety and commotion must have filled the most memorable day of their lives for youthful residents. Men in uniforms performing unknown tasks, possibly their fathers, must have delighted these children. (EC.)

Ridgway had to begin again. Everything was to be imagined. Workers are already beginning the task of cleaning up as the rubble continues to smoke. Roadways had to be cleared for excavation vehicles to begin their work. Men in suits are busy watching workers at their labors. Note the streets were brick at the time. This is the edge of the fire between the destroyed area and buildings that survived. (EC.)

Piles of rubble were everywhere as cleanup began. Standing atop piles of smoking rubble for a photograph was a common activity at the time. The streets were avenues of mud. Note that a fire hose travels down this street and is attached to a fire hydrant on the right. Fire hydrants are not usually appreciated until they are needed. (EC.)

The fire could have been worse. As is apparent in this photograph, the fire did not cross Main Street and threaten the Elk County Courthouse, whose tower is visible in the background here. The courthouse is one of the significant architectural gems of Elk County and survived the fire unscathed. Across the street, a maelstrom of chaos was the scene. Only labyrinths of ruined stone, charred wood, and mud were left. (EC.)

Ironically, Ridgway had a big celebration planned only three days after the fire. The International Order of Oddfellows was a fraternal organization that had clubhouses and sponsored parades. Here, the parade marches past the Elk County Courthouse on Main Street as a large crowd stands witness. In the background, smoking ruins and gaping holes litter the cityscape. A burning ring of fire threatened the town but the town came together and the circle was unbroken. (EC.)

Before the East Branch (of the Clarion River) Dam was built in 1952, Ridgway suffered from flooding. Gallagher Run joins Elk Creek right before Elk Creek joins the Clarion River. The Hyde-Murphy Company complex sat right beside Elk Creek before the Clarion River. This ice floe field shows the yearly winter thaw problem for the business, with the Elk County Courthouse tower also visible at right. (EC.)

Ridgway is seen today from Osterhout Hill. Elk Creek is flowing past the Pennsylvania Railroad station to join the Clarion River at top right. The Hyde-Murphy Company complex stood to the left or south of Elk Creek. Today, Elk Creek has been channelized to prevent flooding. Timber, Elk County's bounty, once again graces the hills that embrace the town. (Dennis McGeehan.)

Here is a view of the north side of Ridgway's Main Street before 1910. Ridgway had three tall buildings with triangular cornice peaks, shown here on the right. On the left is the intersection of Main and North Mill Streets. Only low buildings are seen. A decorative floral arch decorates Main Street. (EC.)

This same view is still from before 1910, but now there is another tall building at far left at the corner of Main and North Mill Streets. That building, at 201 Main Street, today houses the Ling Ling Chinese Restaurant. This block was about to be engulfed by the great fire of the Hyde-Murphy Company in 1910. (EC.)

Looking down Main Street west from Broad Street, the area of the fire and how it burned through from Race to Main Streets is apparent. What could be saved and how much redevelopment would be needed was just starting to be calculated. Many of Ridgway's beautiful commercial buildings would live on. Here, fire hoses still snake over the streets. The Elk County National Bank at Main and North Broad Streets is at right. (EC.)

Ridgway still shows the results of that seminal event today. The three tall buildings at right center survived the fire. Just to the left of that, the fire burned through from Race Street to Main Street. Those buildings had to be replaced. The taller building at left on the corner of Mill and Main Streets, at 201 Main Street, survived the 1910 fire and another in 2011. (Dennis McGeehan.)

Onlookers view the smoking ruins of the Hyde-Murphy Company fire. The conflagration spread from Race Street to Main Street and consumed buildings on the main thoroughfare of the town's central business district. Many wondered how many buildings could be saved and what the new Main Street would look like. The horse at left is stoic. (EC.)

Today, Ridgway is in the National Historic Register. The buildings on Main Street have been carefully restored and decorated with colorful paint schemes. Most feature fancy, decorative overhung cornices that make the street a feast for the eyes. Now, visitors can enjoy a sidewalk café or just stroll to enjoy the sights. Tourism is now a staple of Ridgway's economy. (Dennis McGeehan.)

This postcard view of Main Street shows the block after the great fire. The 201 Main Street Building is on the left on the corner of Main and North Mill Streets. New buildings have been erected to the right and further up Main Street, and the tall buildings up to North Broad Street are unchanged. The "EAT" sign was for a restaurant in the Salberg/Ross Hotel on the south side of Main Street. (MW.)

The 201 Main Street Building, at left, was saved. Fire has consumed most of the buildings between there and the Candy Kitchen at right. The Candy Kitchen's sign has fallen. Imagine the effect of intense heat on candy. Officials confer on what steps to take to begin the long road back from the fire, standing amidst firehoses and water-filled streets as the smoke rose. (EC.)

This is the same view as the previous image, today. The 201 Main Street Building, at left, survived, but all the buildings to the right were rebuilt after the fire. These businesses today are thriving, and the facades are colorful and beautiful architectural examples of the Ridgway Historic District. The cornices are especially detailed and interesting. (Dennis McGeehan.)

Mark Twain once said, "History doesn't repeat itself, but it often rhymes." History and irony are first cousins. On March 19, 2011, the building at 201 Main Street caught fire. Smoke and déjà vu filled the air as historians and senior citizens recalled the great Hyde-Murphy Company fire on the same block. Newer, more modern firefighting equipment made all the difference. (EC.)

Ridgway has a modern fire department with up-to-date equipment and trained volunteers. The 2011 fire was contained and kept to only one building. The beautifully restored buildings that were built after the great fire of 1910 were saved. History does not have to repeat itself. Lessons of the past were learned. (EC.)

Here is the same scene in 2007. Many of the buildings in downtown Ridgway are now part of the National Register Historic District, and the beautiful and colorful architecture has been restored and developed as a tourism draw. The 201 Main Street Building is at left on the corner with a beautiful, fancy cornice. (Dennis McGeehan.)

Eight

Fire in the Sky

The east end of Main Street in Ridgway was graced by mansions of the Murphy family (turret building on left) and Hyde families (building with an arched stone porch on the right). The mansion in front of that was the residence of J.K.P. Hall, another prominent entrepreneur of Elk County. Boot Jack Hill is in the background where Route 219 descends the steep slope. The Murphy mansion was formerly the McCauley mansion. (EC.)

The McCauley mansion was built by tannery executive Calvin McCauley in 1891. McCauley owned the OB Grant Tannery and the Eagle Valley Tannery. He sold both to the US Leather Company, which he then worked for. The mansion was built of brownstone shipped from Buffalo, New York. In the background right is Boot Jack Hill; a steep highway descends this hill and ends here at the end of East Main Street. (EC.)

The McCauley mansion is shown with a surrey for ladies' afternoon riding and a hostler holding the reins. The Gay Nineties featured bonnets and parasols for women. On the left is a jaunty horse cart for children. A bemused observer on the steps watches the fun, while a dog hopes for a ride. Sammy Murphy bought this mansion in 1923. (EC.)

In this scene, the iron horse has replaced the oat horse, but walking is still practiced, as evidenced by the pedestrians passing by the mansion. The home was surrounded by stately shade trees. The man at right is probably a gardener for the estate. This scene is from around the time that Murphy bought the mansion. (EC.)

Behind the mansion was a formal Italian sitting garden that was profuse with decorative flowers that were constantly and meticulously cared for by professional gardeners. The home also had climbing vines covering parts of the building. A garage/gardening house sat at the back of the property. Ridgway residents were always awed by the seasonal blooms of the lush foliage. Floral walkways delighted strolling visitors. (EC.)

Manicured lawns were bordered with flower banks. A birdbath enhanced an archway into a grove of flowering trees. Decorative fences were designed for climbing floral displays. The garden was a treat for the senses. Besides the visual panorama, the garden combined an aroma of flowering plants for a unique sensual experience. The mansion was a private arboretum. (MW.)

The McCauley-Murphy mansion grounds were a perfect place for quiet contemplation and scenic enjoyment. Concrete benches set amidst the garden invited guests to enjoy the botanical elegance. If it rained, there was even a Classical-style gazebo for shelter from the storm. Exotic and native trees were strategically placed around the garden to attract the eye and shade visitors. The overall effect was spectacular. (MW.)

The rectangular gazebo in the McCauley Murphy mansion garden had a fountain that featured running water from a decorative spigot. The garden was designed with multiple layers that guided visitors to different parts of the oasis of green. Brick walkways and stone steps led visitors from terrace to terrace toward ever-changing views. Flowers and trees were designed to achieve a layered effect. (MW.)

On December 15, 1956, a truck lost its brakes on Boot Jack Hill and rolled onto Main Street out of control. Boot Jack Hill was well known for this propensity for runaway trucks, and this incident became the most famous wreck on the hill. The truck smashed into the Samuel Murphy mansion, and chaos ensued. The Murphy family was inside at the time and had to be rescued by firefighters. (EC.)

Firefighters responded to the crash quickly but could not prevent tragedy. The driver of the truck was killed, and the truck demolished. The structure was set ablaze, and the interior was completely destroyed. The building eventually had to be razed. The loss to Ridgway was noteworthy because the town lost one of its most beautiful homes, which was also the home of the president of the town's premier industry. (EC.)

An overturned truck, rising flames, smoking ruins, and a fierce dousing of water from firefighters' hoses created a surreal spectacle on Main Street. A large crowd gathered 10 days before Christmas to witness the tragedy. In the background is the mansion of Harry R. Hyde, a relative of Hyde-Murphy Company co-founder Joseph S. Hyde, at the corner of East Avenue and Main Street. (EC.)

Smoke billows from the burning truck that crashed into the side of the Murphy Mansion. Boot Jack Hill was well known for dangerous runaway trucks, as Route 219 was a steep hill leading directly into the heart of town. As a result of this incident, runaway truck ramps were built that somewhat alleviated the problem, and finally, in 1990, a bypass was built so trucks no longer had to use the hill. (EC.)

After the body of the truck driver was removed, the truck continued to burn and was extinguished. The wreckage of the truck was in the way of firefighters, so workers here are attempting to right the trailer and remove it so firefighters can fight the blaze raging inside the mansion. The Murphy family was rescued from the building, and then firefighters vainly attempted to save the structure. (EC.)

Imagine the view of a youth standing on Ridgway's Main Street witnessing this spectacular scene. Fire hoses snake along the town's main thoroughfare. Multiple ladders climb the structure to get at the blaze inside. Smoke and water completely obscure the top of the familiar building. A large crowd excitedly observes the surreal scene and speculates. It could inspire a youth to dream of becoming a fireman. (EC.)

Ladder fire trucks and individual ladders scale the building to fight the inferno that was raging inside both the ground floor and the upper story. Firemen climb the ladders to use the windows to direct fire hoses. A wooden structure may have been feared to collapse, but this stone building appears to be still structurally sound at the moment. Onlookers and fire department personnel appear to be planning strategy. (EC.)

Here, the fire has spread to the attic level, and the mounted truck ladder is employed to deliver water to the very top of the house. The fireman at the top of the ladder has a critical and specialized job. This is why fire department volunteers are highly trained for just such an emergency even though they hope that the skill may never be needed. (EC.)

The entire structure is now smoke-filled, and firefighters can only speculate on what they may find inside. An observer may start to wonder about the future of one of Ridgway's signature mansions. The beautiful interior wood art of the Hyde-Murphy Company did not survive. The building had to be destroyed, and only an empty lot full of memories remained. (EC.)

A dynamic action scene is captured here. At this moment, a truck ladder fireman is directing a water stream into the upper-story windows while four firemen anxiously wait for results on the roof of the porch. Smoke billows everywhere, obscuring the progress or lack of progress on the blaze. Sure-footedness and no fear of heights is a job requirement here. (EC.)

A fireman in the sky and fire in the sky is the subject of this photograph. Getting above the flames and directing water on the best spot is the job of this volunteer fireman. The elegant mansion is being consumed from the inside out. An architectural gem is being lost to an unanticipated twist of fate. Fire is devastating, and so is water. The mansion succumbed to both. (EC.)

Nine

Lilies of the Valley

The Harry R. Hyde residence (built in 1896) is on East Avenue, built in the Queen Anne Victorian style. He was the grandson of Joseph S. Hyde. The house was built on the site of an early log cabin of pioneer James Gallagher. It has a massive English-style great hall with an oversized fireplace and an oak-paneled staircase. An enclosed porch is accented with leaded art glass windows. (Dennis McGeehan.)

This is Calvin Hudson McCauley and his wife Juliette McGibney McCauley in front of their stately mansion built in 1893. Samuel Murphy bought the McCauley mansion in 1923 and lived there with his family for the next 33 years. He was the son of Hyde-Murphy Company co-founder Walter P. Murphy and was also the company general manager. The interior woodwork was designed by the Hyde-Murphy Company. Note the wide wrap-around porch with a Romanesque entry arch and sturdy supporting Doric columns. The building was destroyed by fire in 1956. (EC.)

Elizabeth Kime Hyde was the widow of Pennsylvania state senator William Henry Hyde. She built this mansion in 1907 on the corner of Main Street and East Avenue. The Hyde family was involved in the timber industry developed by Joseph S. Hyde, founder of the Hyde-Murphy Company. Their high-quality woodwork is displayed in the interior of this massive Richardsonian Romanesque style mansion. A grand staircase leads to a third-floor ballroom. (Dennis McGeehan.)

John G. Whitmore was an attorney for the Pennsylvania Railroad and the Baltimore & Ohio Railroad. He was appointed to the Superior Court of Pennsylvania. He built this house in 1898 in the Queen Anne Victorian style on East Avenue. The home has a gentleman's game room in the basement and massive carved woodwork throughout. An adjacent carriage house features a lift for buggies and stables for horses. (Dennis McGeehan.)

Madison S. Kline built this Colonial Revival–style home on Center Street in 1903. Kline was a banker and manager of the Russell Snow Plow Company. The home was later acquired by the J.K.P. Hall family, a prominent Ridgway family. Tall Ionic columns support a third-floor ballroom. Since 1922, the building has served as the Ridgway Public Library. (Dennis McGeehan.)

This eclectic Shingle-style residence was built by Harry Thayer in 1906 on Center Street. Harry Thayer was the grandson of early Ridgway pioneer David Thayer. Harry operated a hotel, the Exchange (later Clarion) House on the Clarion River. He also managed the Laurel Mill lumber mill for his father, Henry. In 1942, Walter P. Murphy bought the house for his two daughters Kathryn and Elizabeth. (Dennis McGeehan.)

Abraham Lincoln Bell was a schoolteacher who moved to Ridgway and became the president and general manager of the J.H. McEwen Manufacturing Company (later Ridgway Dynamo and Engine Company). He served on the Ridgway School Board and helped found the Ridgway YMCA. Built in 1904 in the Georgian Colonial style on South Street, the home features a semi-circular porch supported by Doric columns. (Dennis McGeehan.)

Frank Clawson built this Georgian Revival style house on Hyde Avenue in 1907. He made his fortune at the Clawson Chemical Company in Hallton, supplying chemicals to the tannery industry. The paneled and beamed living room stretches the entire depth of the house and is designed for large social gatherings. Multiple dormer windows grace the roofline. The larger Palladian-style window is above the semi-circular porch entryway. (Dennis McGeehan.)

William Moore built this home in the Eclectic style in 1909 on Hyde Avenue as a wedding present for his son. The house features a large wrap-around porch and unique twin upper stories. One side is a traditional gabled structure, and the other is a three-story octagonal tower. The interior features built-in wooden bookcases, china cabinets, paneled walls, and a beamed ceiling. (Dennis McGeehan.)

Charles A. Kline worked for the Hyde-Murphy Company as a manager. This Tudor Revival–style house was designed by Henry C. Park, Hyde-Murphy's resident architect, in 1907 on Hyde Avenue. Kline died unexpectedly just before he was to move into his new home. The house was owned for some time by John Merton Flynn of the Elliott Company. (Dennis McGeehan.)

Jackson S. Schultz was the vice president of the Elk Tanning Company. The company owned 45 tanneries and employed 6,000 workers. They marketed shoe leather throughout America and Europe. The American Foursquare–style house was built in 1917 on South Street. The house features Hyde-Murphy oak woodwork. The buff brick house shows the trend away from the ornate styles of the past toward plainness and functionality. (Dennis McGeehan.)

Jerome Powell came to Ridgway to found the *Elk County Advocate* newspaper, the forerunner of the current *Ridgway Record*. Powell proceeded to amass a fortune in lumber, mercantile, land, and real estate investments. The mansion was built in 1865 in the Italian Villa style on South Street. The building is surmounted by a belvedere. The large wrap-around porch includes an attached gazebo. (Dennis McGeehan.)

Edgar Powell, the son of Jerome Powell, built this house beside his father's on South Street in 1903 in the late-Victorian Eclectic style. Edgar served as Ridgway's mayor. The buff brick mansion features a dramatically curved staircase inside. The diverse exterior features multiple fenestrations, including half-moon windows and bull's-eye windows, both horizontal and vertical style. (Dennis McGeehan.)

This French Second Empire–style house with a mansard roof was built by Fred Schoening on South Street in 1875. The house was updated in the late 19th century with Colonial Revival additions of a columned and turreted front porch and art glass windows. Fred Schoening organized Company H, 16th Regiment of the Pennsylvania National Guard, which he commanded for 10 years. He was later involved in the music business. (Dennis McGeehan.)

Burr Cartwright was one of Elk County's wealthiest residents. He made a fortune in timber, coal, brick, and railroads in the Toby Valley. He went bankrupt, then worked for the Hall Company, and later returned to Buffalo, where he was again successful. He built this mansion on Center Street in 1900 in the late Victorian Eclectic style. The third-floor ballroom is the largest and most opulent in town. (Dennis McGeehan.)

Byron F. Ely was one of Ridgway's earliest lumbermen. His lumberyard was along Elk Creek on what is today Front Street. This Queen Anne–style house was built on Center Street in 1888. The house includes a grand Eastlake-style staircase illuminated by beveled, leaded art glass windows. Ely died shortly after occupying his new home. (Dennis McGeehan.)

Perry S. Smith began as a tanner. He built a tannery with his brothers in Arroyo and later became vice president of the Elk Tanning Company. He and his brothers founded the Smith Brothers Department Store in the Grand Central Building on Main Street. His home features a grand ballroom and Hyde-Murphy woodwork. The house was built on Center Street in 1896 in the late Victorian Eclectic style. (Dennis McGeehan.)

Beverly P. Mercer built this buff brick house on Center Street in 1896 in the Victorian Vernacular style. He operated a meat market on Main Street. The house was later owned by Madison J. Beach, president of the Elk Tanning Company. Beach added the large cut-stone front porch and a carved chestnut staircase with art glass windows. The house features brown brick quoins. (Dennis McGeehan.)

The Elder Campbell house was built in the Queen Anne/Eastlake style on Center Street in 1886. It is a simple clapboard house originally built for Elder Campbell, owner of the Eagle Valley Store with William H. Osterhout. Campbell also cut timber for the Elk Tanning Company. Interior renovations added value to the house, and the structure was eventually narrowly saved from demolition. (Dennis McGeehan.)

George Dixon was a lawyer, educator, and local businessman and served in the Pennsylvania Assembly for four terms. He built this Shingle-style Victorian cottage in 1888 on Center Street. The interior features a cherry staircase. Note the third-floor enclosed sleeping porch on top of the bay/turret. The curbside still has a carriage stone. (Dennis McGeehan.)

Homer B. Norton was an engineer who designed Ridgway's clean water supply. Norton rebuilt this house around an earlier structure. It was designed in the late Victorian Mission style in 1916 on Center Street. The interior combines Victorian with Arts and Crafts style. The third floor is a single room with no visible support, using the exterior walls to cantilever the entire weight of the roof. (Dennis McGeehan.)

William C. Healy came to Ridgway to work for the Dickinson lumber company. He soon purchased the Laurel Mill lumber operation. He built this Queen Anne/Stick–style mansion on Montmorenci Avenue in 1888. The scenic, complex, multichromatic exterior is visually exciting. It has a grand staircase in the Eastlake style. The original shutters are operated by cranks from inside. (Dennis McGeehan.)

George E. Dickinson was a very early lumberman. He built this house on West Main Street in 1855. It is the only surviving example of the Greek Revival style in Ridgway. The central portion of the house has pilasters supporting a Greek pediment that surrounds a triangular window. The aspect of the house resembles a simple Greek temple. (Dennis McGeehan.)

James Knox Polk Hall was a state senator and important businessman in many fields, including timber, railroads, banking, and real estate. His mansion in the Victorian style on East Main Street was a showplace. Hall, his wife Kate, and her mother Jane Hyde are seen on the porch. Note the lush greenery decorating the home, including the second-floor porch and the inscribed carriage stone at curbside. (EC.)

The James Knox Polk Hall mansion on East Main Street has undergone cosmetic changes but has similar touches. It still is decorated with floral displays. Today, the building is the home of the Ridgway American Legion. The second-floor porch is still open. The tympanum inside the porch pediment has been replaced with plain wood paneling. The roofline includes decorative terra cotta moldings. (Dennis McGeehan.)

Henry Shimmelfeng was a lumberman who ran mills at Straight and Instanter. He built this mansion on South Mill Street in 1903 in the Colonial Revival style. The orange brick building includes several gables and a third-floor dormer window. It includes a cut-stone wrap-around porch. Today, the mansion is the home of the Ridgway Elks Lodge. (Dennis McGeehan.)

The David G. Messenger house is today South Street Botanical Designs. The building has a redbrick first floor and a shingle second floor, with a third floor attic, including three dormer windows. A wide front porch with Doric columns graces the entrance, and a porte cochere is on the east side. The fenestration of this house is varied, with beveled glass, metal screens, and designs. Topiaries add interesting landscape features. (Dennis McGeehan.)

David Robertson was the superintendent of the Northwestern Mining & Exchange coalfields in Fox Township. He built this turreted Victorian Shingle-style mansion on Center Street in 1891. The first floor is red brick, while the upper stories are buff shingle clad. Since the roof has grey shingles, the overall effect is polychromatic by levels. Front windows are recessed and include a bull's-eye window. Note the fancy script "R" in the porch pediment. (Dennis McGeehan.)

This frame house on a rough-cut stone foundation used to be the Van Aken Funeral Home and is today the Krise Funeral Home. It is a large multi-gabled building with a small side porch and second-story portico. The ground floor front has three triple windows, each surmounted with a fancy fanlight. The building has an offset square tower. (Dennis McGeehan.)

Oscar B. Grant founded the Grant-Horton Tannery on the Clarion River right below his mansion here on West Main Street in 1867 in the Victorian Clapboard style. The home has a large wrap-around porch, which includes a built-in gazebo topped by a fancy finial. The gable pediment has an ornate multi-point star window under bracketed overhanging eaves. (Dennis McGeehan.)

Norman T. Arnold built the Bonifels mansion in 1898 on a vista overlooking Ridgway. It was built of Vermont greystone, delivered by rail, hauled up the mountain by wagon, and cut on site. The home features a conical stone tower and a crenelated cornerstone tower. The hipped roof also has hipped roof dormers. It has an extended entrance porch and side porte cochere. The roofline is surmounted by decorative ironwork. (EC.)

The interior of Bonifels was just as fancy as the exterior. This view is from the entrance foyer into a sitting room. On the left is the beautiful carved wooden staircase. The space includes intricate, beautifully carved upholstered wooden chairs. An exotic decorative planter is at left. Note the fancy light fixtures. (EC.)

This sitting room includes wicker furniture, rocking chairs, and a brick fireplace. End tables and fern planters accent the room, which has heavy decorative draperies. Fancy wallpaper adds artistry. Mirrors and still-life paintings adorn the walls. The room is overlooked by the bust of an unknown person. (EC.)

The library has a heavy, darker look with wood paneling, including wood-paneled beams. Leather upholstered chairs invite perusing the many volumes inside the built-in glass-encased wooden bookcase. A fancy reading light looks like the books on the table are in use. On top of the bookcase are a bell jar timepiece and two busts. Shakespeare looks on from the left, while the right bust is hidden. (EC.)

The music room was an essential room in any mansion. Private musical performances were popular before radio and television. Long nights were enjoyed with the lively strains of classical and popular music. In this music room, a piano and guitar are evident. The room looks well used, as sheet music is still open on the stand. (EC.)

All mansions had to have a fancy dining room for every day and for entertaining. This dining room is set for a meal. Typical dining room furniture included a china hutch, credenza or cabinet, a sideboard or buffet, flatware drawers, and a stemware cupboard. This dining room had an ornate chandelier, tasteful draperies, linen tablecloth, crystal, and silver servers. Another thing that all elegant mansions prided themselves on was decorative fresh flowers. (EC.)

Old fashioned mansions often had separate rooms for men and women. After dinner, gentlemen usually retired to a drawing room for port wine and cigars and to discuss business and politics. Women usually retired to a more feminine sitting room to discuss domestic politics. Overstuffed loveseats, needlepoint pillows, and fancy carved wood tables and footstools may have been evident. Statuary and artwork were common. Gone are the days. (EC.)

The entrance foyer at Bonifels led to this beautiful carved wooden stairway. The floor, walls, and stairs were all highly decorated. The ceiling was beautifully decorative. Exposed wood-paneled beams create a coffered ceiling that adds beauty and height to the space. Potted plants and a coat rack are handy, as is a loveseat for visitors. The banister newel post is a full-figure Greek nude holding aloft a staff. (EC.)

This is the view from the Bonifels mansion into the valley of the lilies. Many of the beautiful mansions of Ridgway are in this view. The hills of Ridgway are once again forested with the lumber that gave prosperity to this valley. Note how many trees grace the downtown. Ironically, note the truck on Boot Jack Hill, now with a descending lane for trucks to avoid the downtown. (Dennis McGeehan.)

Ten

SAWDUST AND ICE

Wood made Ridgway's prosperity. Woodcutting was an art, and the crosscut saw and double-bitted ax were the woodhicks' tools. In the late 19th century, huge forests were leveled one tree at a time by this tool and two men. These men are similar—maybe even twins. The trees were as strong as the men, but the lumberjacks eventually prevailed, and Penn's Woods was clearcut. (SM.)

In this scene from 1931, the big trees had vanished, but the crosscut was still active. These woodcutters may have been deer hunters who populated the Pennsylvania forests that were regenerating. Deer camps grew rapidly, and each camp needed firewood. Deer were scarce in the mature crown forest but proliferated in the growing second-growth forests that were returning. (EC.)

This county employee is pruning trees in front of the Elk County Courthouse in the late 20th century. Power saws have replaced the two-man crosscut saw. He has no idea that this activity would become Ridgway's new signature celebration. In 2000, Ridgway inaugurated the Chainsaw Carvers Rendezvous, and wood returned as Ridgway's famous commodity. (EC.)

The Hyde-Murphy Company, famous for wood mill workers, went out of business after 77 years of high-quality woodworking. In 2000, woodworking artists from around the world came to Ridgway to display their skills with chainsaws. Visitors can watch the art being created. Pieces of their handicraft are auctioned off to benefit charity, and it is now the signature event on Ridgway's social calendar. (Dennis McGeehan.)

How much wood could a wooden woodcarver carve at the Ridgway Borough Office? Visitors to the Rendezvous purchase sculptures, and many of them remain local. Ridgway has bloomed with wooden artwork from the Chainsaw Carvers Rendezvous. The town has become an outdoor sculpture museum, with carvings decorating many streets, gardens, and lawns. The effect is a tribute to the woodworking fame of the Hyde-Murphy Company, Ridgway's most famous business. (Dennis McGeehan.)

If one finds a totem pole somewhere other than Alaska, they may be in Ridgway. Animals, mythical figures, and hard to describe wooden artwork can be experienced all around Ridgway. It has all benefited charity. Also visible all around town are loaded log trucks navigating the streets. Renewable forests still generate income for the community. (Dennis McGeehan.)

A chainsaw woodcarver, carved from ice, greets visitors to the Chainsaw Carvers Rendezvous in front of the Ridgway Chamber of Commerce. Besides wood, ice carving has become a staple of the event. This temporary artwork is a beautiful contrast to the more lasting wooden pieces. Children love the ice sculptures and marvel at how chainsaws can carve ice into such beautiful creations. (Dennis McGeehan.)

The size and shape of the wood carvings are truly awe-inspiring. Some are incredibly complex and decorative. Hundreds of pieces are scattered throughout the festival, and visitors buy and bid on many. Souvenirs and fair food are available, and photography is in full season. Any visitor can imagine she is the queen of the Rendezvous. (Dennis McGeehan.)

Fire and ice fill Ridgway's past. South Main Street, the scene of the great Hyde-Murphy Company fire in 1910, is a reminder of the water that was essential to Ridgway's prosperity. Water transported wood in the past. It also fought fires. Today, water carries tourists on the Clarion Wild & Scenic River through the woods of the Allegheny National Forest, the Pennsylvania Lumber Heritage Region, and the Pennsylvania wilds. (Dennis McGeehan.)